Contents

A cycle of changes

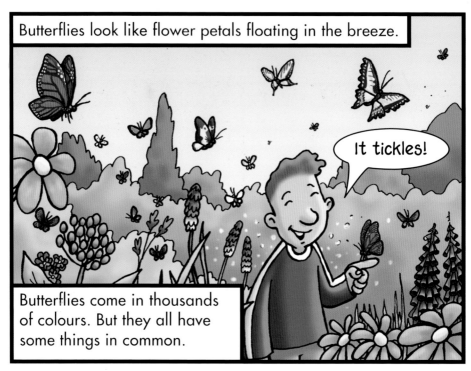

Butterflies look like flower petals floating in the breeze.

It tickles!

Butterflies come in thousands of colours. But they all have some things in common.

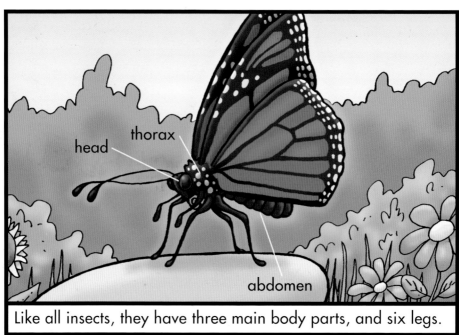

head

thorax

abdomen

Like all insects, they have three main body parts, and six legs.

A hard exoskeleton covers their body.

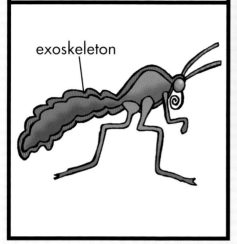

exoskeleton

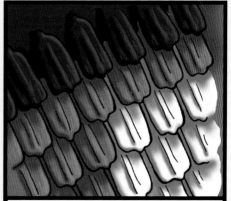

Their wing colours come from tiny scales. Monarch butterflies have black and orange wings.

But monarchs and other butterflies don't start their lives with wings.

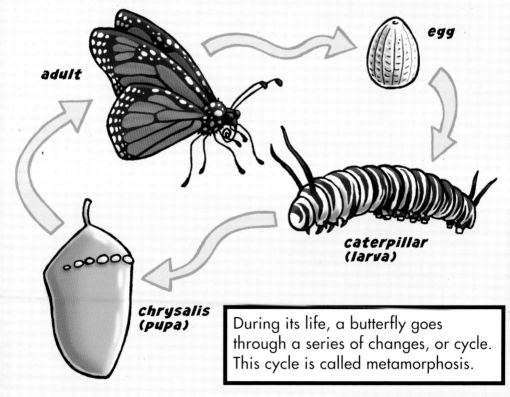

egg

adult

caterpillar
(larva)

chrysalis
(pupa)

During its life, a butterfly goes through a series of changes, or cycle. This cycle is called metamorphosis.

The cycle begins as a female monarch lays eggs. She puts them on milkweed plants, just one egg per leaf.

Each egg is as tiny as the head of a pin.

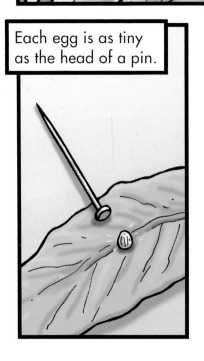

After about three days, something chews a hole from inside the egg.

The tiny creature crawls its way out.

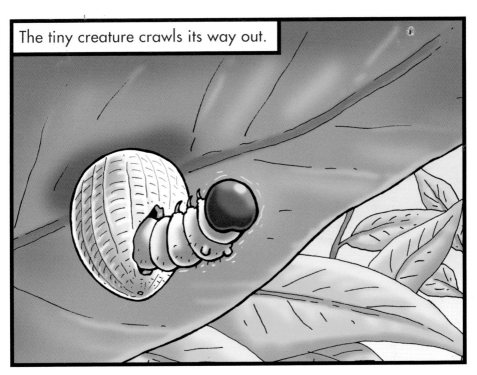

The creature looks like a worm with many little feet. It's called a caterpillar, or larva.

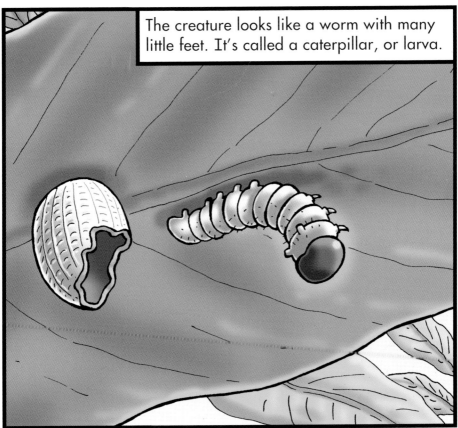

The growing caterpillar

A caterpillar eats and eats. Its eggshell is the first thing on the menu.

Crunch!

Then it eats the leaf where it was born.

The caterpillar gets stronger. It crawls to other leaves to find food.

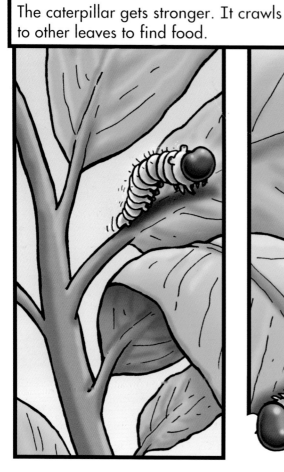

Young caterpillars face dangers. At first, they are so small that a drop of rain could wash them away.

Spiders and other minibeasts hunt and eat caterpillars.

Caterpillars have one defence. The milkweed they eat makes them poisonous.

Some birds and mice get ill after eating them. They know to stay away from these caterpillars.

As the caterpillar eats, it gets fatter.
Soon its skin gets too tight, and splits.

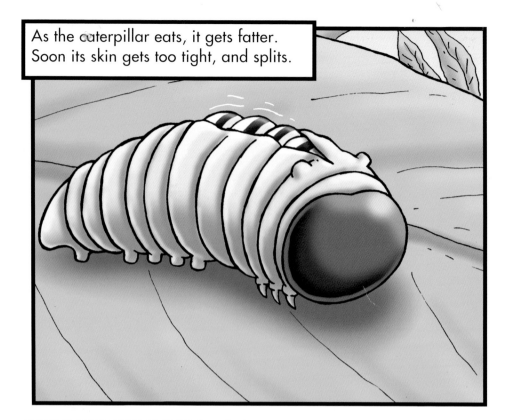

The caterpillar crawls out. A new, loose skin covers it now.

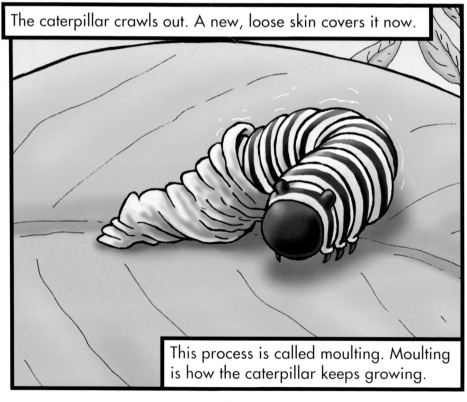

This process is called moulting. Moulting
is how the caterpillar keeps growing.

The caterpillar eats, grows, and moults for about three weeks. A monarch caterpillar moults five times.

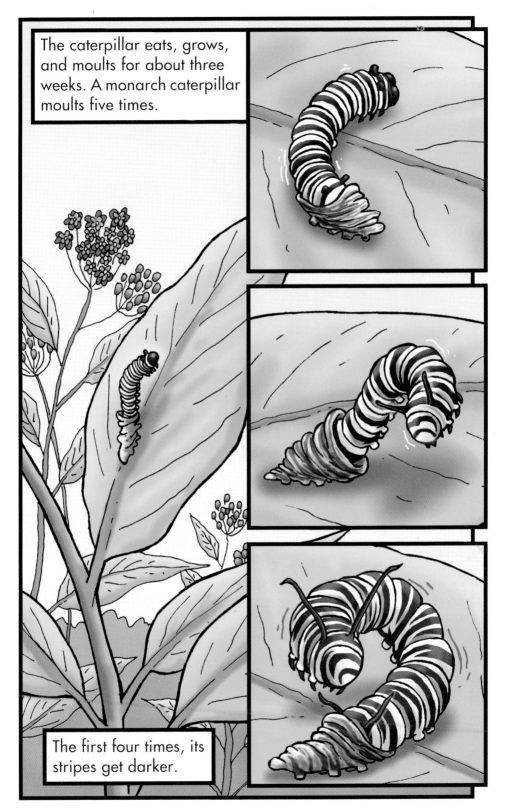

The first four times, its stripes get darker.

The fifth moult is special. The caterpillar finds a branch. It spins a small pad of silk.

The caterpillar grabs onto the silk with tiny hooks on its feet. It hangs upside down.

Then the caterpillar moults. This time, the caterpillar looks light green.

The caterpillar's new skin gets hard, like a shell.

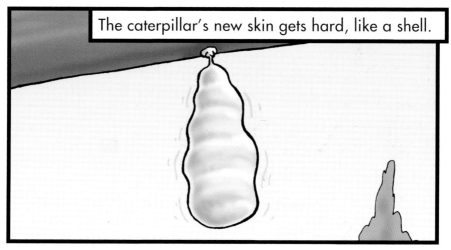

Now the caterpillar is called a chrysalis, or pupa. A monarch chrysalis is shiny with gold spots.

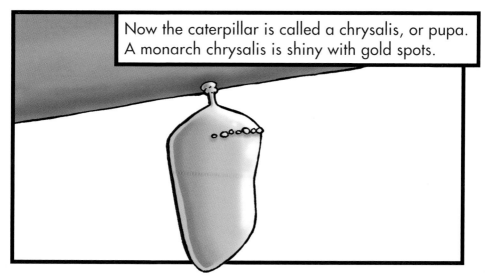

Inside the chrysalis, wings, legs, and other adult body parts are growing. After 10 days, the chrysalis seems to lose colour.

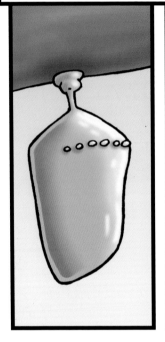

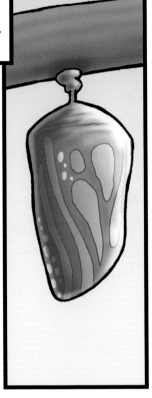

By the end, the chrysalis becomes clear. The next step is about to begin.

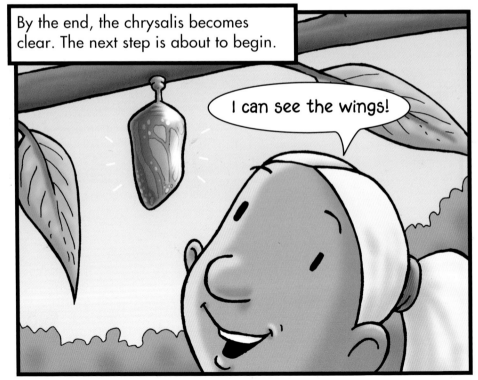

I can see the wings!

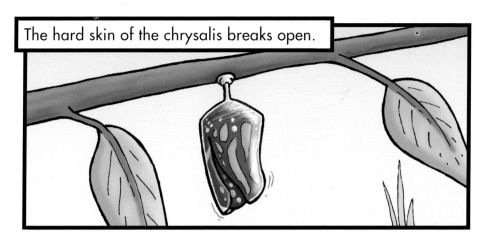

The hard skin of the chrysalis breaks open.

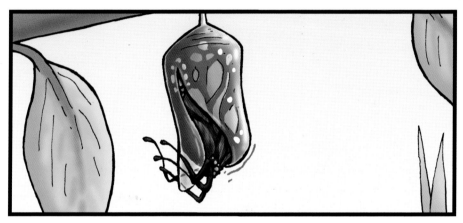

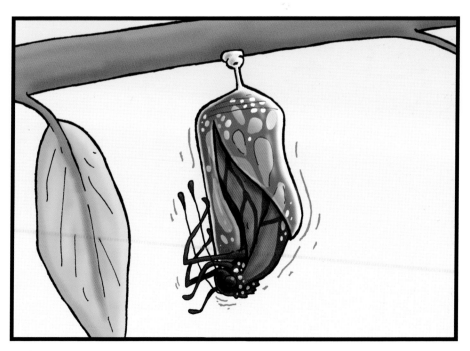

The adult butterfly

At last, the adult monarch butterfly climbs out. The metamorphosis is complete!

The damp butterfly has flat, folded wings. It cannot fly until its wings are open and dry.

This is a dangerous time. Birds may catch the butterfly and eat it.

But the monarch's bold colour warns birds to stay away. The adult is poisonous, just like the caterpillar.

17

Slowly, the monarch's wings unfold.

The butterfly flies away to find food.

18

Butterflies get food from flowers. Flowers make a sweet liquid called nectar.

A butterfly drinks nectar through a tube-like mouthpart called a proboscis.

proboscis

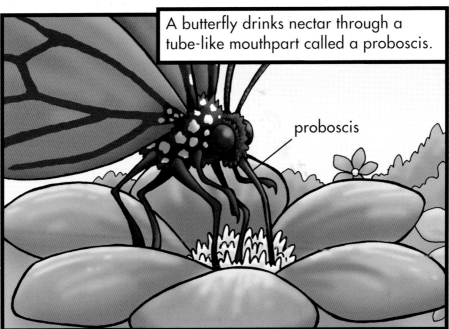

Adult monarchs born in spring and summer live for a few weeks. Monarchs born in autumn migrate south to escape cold weather. They live until the next spring.

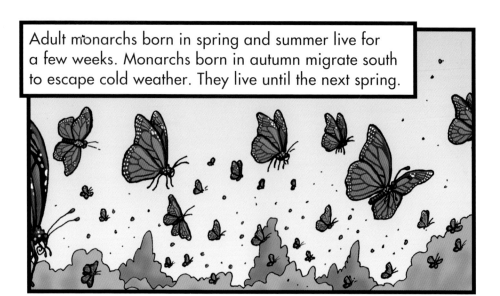

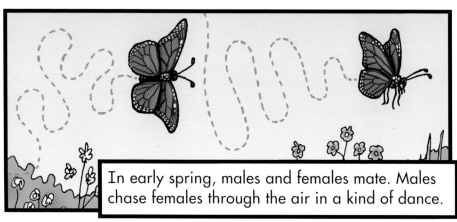

In early spring, males and females mate. Males chase females through the air in a kind of dance.

There will be more monarchs soon!

The monarchs return north in spring. The female finds a milkweed plant where she lays her eggs.

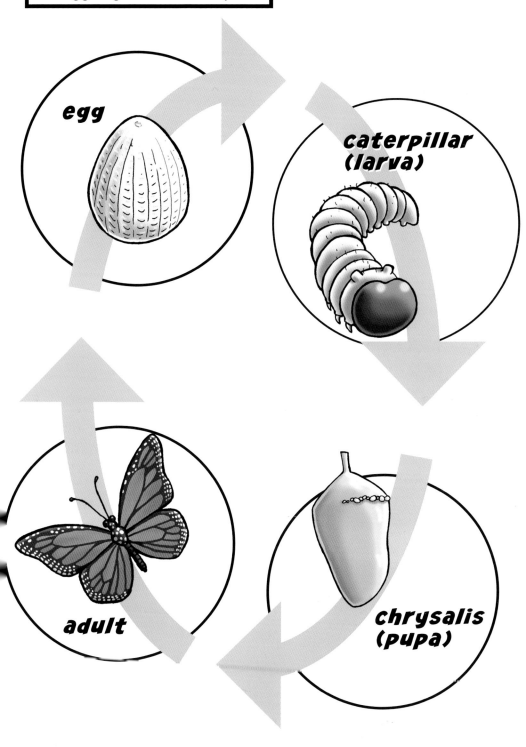

The egg begins a new life cycle.

egg

caterpillar (larva)

adult

chrysalis (pupa)

Glossary

chrysalis the third life stage of a butterfly. Pupa is another word for chrysalis.

exoskeleton hard outer shell of an insect. The exoskeleton covers and protects the insect.

larva insect at the stage in its life cycle between an egg and a pupa. Butterfly larvae are also called caterpillars.

metamorphosis series of changes some animals go through as they develop from eggs to adults

migrate to move from one place to another when seasons change or when food runs out

moult to shed an outer layer of skin, or exoskeleton, so a new exoskeleton can be seen

nectar sweet liquid made by many kinds of flowers. Butterflies drink nectar.

proboscis long, tube-shaped mouthpart. A butterfly uses its proboscis to drink nectar.

pupa insect at the stage in its life cycle between larva and adult. For butterflies, chrysalis is another word for pupa.

Find out more

Books

Caterpillars to Butterflies, Bobbie Calman (Crabtree, 2009)

From Caterpillar to Butterfly (Following the Life Cycle), Suzanne Slade (Picture Window Books, 2009)

Life Cycle of a Honeybee, Ruth Thomson (Wayland, 2010)

Nic Bishop Butterflies and Moths, Nic Bishop (Scholastic, 2009)

Websites

http://www.kidsbutterfly.org/life-cycle
Visit this website to learn more about the life cycle of the monarch butterfly.

http://www.britishbutterflies.co.uk/asp/lifecycle.asp
Look at some stunning photos of butterflies and learn more about British butterfly species and the best places to find them.

http://www.ngfl-cymru.org.uk/vtc/minbeasts/eng/Introduction/MainSessionPart2.htm
An interactive website that will help you to remember the stages of a butterfly's life cycle.

Index